MW00943757

Dr. Shaniqua Jones'

RESTORATIVE
Justice
&
RESTORATIVE
Practice

TRAINING MANUAL

Dr. Shaniqua Jones' Restorative Justice & Restorative Practice Training Manual

Excerpts from *Implementing Talking Circles in a Living Learning Community* by Dr. Shaniqua Jones. Reprinted by permission.

Cover & Interior Design: Julie M. Holloway, JMH Cre8ive Solutions
Editor: Tiffany Jasper, Tiff's Editing Café

Books may be purchased by contacting the publisher and author at:
Shaniqua Jones Publishing, LLC
Chicago, IL 60628
Dr. Shaniqua Jones
www.shaniquajones.com

ISBN 978-1542662444

TABLE OF CONTENTS

1

AUTHOR BIOGRAPHY

Dr. Shaniqua Jones, a leader in her own right and a proven professional of high standards within the post-secondary arena, currently works at Trinity Christian College as the Director of Community Engagement and Diversity Programs. She has trained student leaders, staff, faculty, administration, and community members on how to best provide restorative practices.

Dr. Jones is an inspirational author, educator, and Restorative Justice Circle Keeper. She has self-published her first book, *12: A Memoir To My Younger Self* in May 2016 and co-authored two entrepreneurship publications including *The Entrepreneur Within You Volume I* and *Success, Failure and Recovery*. In addition to being a loving wife and raising her five children, she's actively writing or involved in activities relating to collaborative communities and education for young and adult learners.

Dr. Jones was introduced to the philosophy of Restorative Justice (RJ) and Restorative Practices (RP) as a graduate student under the leadership and guidance of her mentor. Her passion for RJ and RP has afforded her the opportunity to train, speak, and present across the Chicagoland area. As a recent doctoral graduate, she applied her knowledge of RJ and RP to share aspects of that journey with others.

Dr. Jones began her professional career in the non-profit sector on the south side of Chicago for several years. During this time, she was promoted from office assistant to executive assistant to head coordinator over three male recovery homes. She formed lasting relationships with a variety of state agencies ranging from Cook County Drug Court, Chicago Department of Public Health, Illinois Department of Human Services, and Illinois Department of Corrections.

Dr. Jones transitioned to entrepreneurship as the CEO of Senorita Entertainment providing a welcoming experience for comedians and patrons to partake in fellowship and laughter in the south suburban Cook County area. The platform allowed local comics to hone their skills while nationally recognized comedians returned to an intimate setting to perform. She saw the need to be more creative in her approach to promoting local talent by combining a vendor experience for small business owners.

She completed her undergraduate and graduate degree at Governor State University (GSU). She learned of the philosophy of Restorative Justice under the leadership of her mentor and professor. Restorative Justice became a way of life for her as she was able to apply theory to practice in her own personal affairs. Shaniqua was recognized as a student leader on campus by modeling the way and encouraging the heart. Even through facing hard times, she managed to rise to the occasion. For her final project to complete her graduate degree, she co-created a 15-semester credit hour Restorative Justice Certificate Program. In 2013, Shaniqua graduated with her Master of Science degree in Criminal Justice, earning the privilege of being the Commencement Speaker which is one of the highest academic honors a student can achieve at GSU.

Her diverse background in academics, her profession as well as her personal journey has allowed her to understand the concerns of those she serve. As a former student, she has had the opportunity to serve the student body as a leader in addressing concerns, being visible and available, and supporting student-based programs on campus.

She completed her doctoral degree in Interdisciplinary Leadership with a specialization in higher education in May 2016. She has become an active restorative and social justice advocate within higher education. Her passion for Restorative Justice has afforded her the opportunity to speak and present across the Chicagoland area on the proactive and reactive approaches regarding restorative practices such as, build meaningful relationships, promoting accountability, and operating in a safe environment.

She plans to work with organizations offering an outlet for youth to speak from the heart without judgment, however receiving support of their creative endeavors. She believes that we are support systems to one another and should exemplify social capital in terms of creating solutions and resolving issues internally. She also recognizes the importance of promoting sustainable consumption in higher education as a contribution to bridge the gap between service learning and subsidiary learning to maximize the academic experience for students as well as administration, faculty and staff.

Dr. Shaniqua Jones understands that education plays a crucial role in the social development of young and returning adults to effectively face societal challenges, cultural diversity, and environmental issues – emphasizing civic engagement. With many educational institutions moving towards a more civically engaged institution, the paradigm shift to focus on social justice and civic responsibility is becoming more prominent. To promote the social and economic development through service and incidental learning, WE must have the opportunity to be catalyst to enhance experiences through collaborative efforts. This quest is continued through Shaniqua's academic, professional and personal gains.

You can visit her at www.shaniquajones.com.

2

PROCLAMATIONS

In 2013, I attended my first Art of Hosting at the beautiful Morton Arboretum in Lisle, Illinois. I experienced a spiritual awakening amongst complete strangers that all desired restoration in the lives of the children we served. Many of the attendees were educators while the others, along with myself, were a part of the Restorative Justice (RJ) community. There were two profound proclamations made that I share every chance I have; especially when facilitating RJ Trainings.

The first profound proclamation is:

THE FOUR PRINCIPLES

1. Whoever comes are the right people.

2. Whatever happens is the only thing that could have.

3. Whenever it starts is the right time.

4. When it is over, it is over.

The second profound proclamation is:

THE LAW OF TWO FEET

If you find yourself in a situation where you are not contributing or learning; move somewhere you can.

Take a moment to think of a proclamation you would like to share with others. Proclamations are considered to be public statements that we would expect others to respect and value.

I realized that when I shared these two proclamations, shareholders were more apt to participate in the facilitated process. For clarity, many in the Restorative Justice community refer to community members as stakeholders. Under the leadership of Dr. Terry Winfrey, President of Prairie State College, I learned to refer to community members as shareholders, also.

The term stakeholder is more appropriate from a business perspective while shareholders compliments the purpose of the restorative process; community.

3

ORGANIZATIONAL OBJECTIVES

1. What is the mission of your organization?

2. What is the vision of your organization?

3. What are the goals of your organization?

4. How does the mission, vision, and goals align with restorative practices?

IMPORTANT QUESTIONS TO ASK:

- What is being implemented?

- What is the quality and fidelity of the implementation?

- How can we improve program implementation and management?

- What activities are being undertaken?

- What outputs result from those activities?

- What are the impacts in court, schools, the community, in families?

- Are there other impacts?

- Are we being successful, cost-effective?

4

KEY DEFINITIONS

- **Restorative Justice** - Restorative justice is a process where all the stakeholders (shareholders) affected by an injustice have an opportunity to discuss how they have been affected by the injustice and to decide what should be done to repair the harm (Braithwaite, 2004). Restorative Justice involves the utilization of collaborative, community-based or community-oriented techniques for responding to crimes and offenses (Karp, 2013).

- **Restorative Practices** - Restorative practices is a social science that studies how to build social capital and achieve social discipline through participatory learning and decision-making (Watchel, 2013).

- **Talking Circles - is an** example of a restorative practice. In a Talking Circle participants explore a particular issue or topic from many different perspectives. Talking Circles do not attempt to reach **consensus** on the topic. Rather, they allow all voices to be respectfully heard and offer participants diverse perspectives to stimulate their reflections (Pranis, 2005).

5

VALUES AND RESPECT

Define values. According to Merriam-Webster, values are defined as the relative worth, utility, or importance.

Define respect. According to the English Oxford Living Dictionaries, respect is defined as a feeling of deep admiration for someone or something elicited by their abilities, qualities, or achievements.

Respect is a two-way street that we must acknowledge in order to build and sustain within our communities. We must be willing and open to the possibilities when we make an intentional effort to build a relationship. Quick question. How do you define community? We can think of how we define communities forming various levels/perspectives: micro, meso and macro. The diagram below displays the three levels that further support the many levels of community we connect. We do not have to be limited to one specific location or demographic.

Hosting challenging conversations in the classroom is no small task, especially when one carries into the conversation strongly held positions or convictions. This training opportunity will model and discuss the way that Talking Circles, a means of cultivating conversations in which all are free to listen and to be heard, can be one practice to aid in the pedagogy of in-depth dialogue.

I will guide this experiential learning session, inviting staff and faculty to participate in a brief Talking Circle and then speaking about the techniques and the soul-work needed to host a Talking Circle well. No preparation is necessary beyond your <u>willingness</u> to attend and participate in the conversation.

6

VALUES EXERCISE – TALKING CIRCLE

- Provide name and something unique about yourself

- List top three personal values

- Describe a time when you felt valued

- Describe a time when you felt unvalued

- Describe the perfect classroom

- How do you engage your students? Has this

  technique been effective?

7

History of Restorative Justice and Restorative Practices

There are various historical backgrounds of Restorative Justice Researchers have exclaimed Restorative Justice deriving from indigenous cultures from thousands of years ago to the Truth and Reconciliation Commission (TRC) of 1995. TRC was organized to help deal with crimes and violence committed under apartheid in efforts to "establish the truth in relation to past events," pursue national unity, reconciliation, and understanding (Truth and Reconciliation Commission, 2003, p.2). TRC presented the true essence of Restorative Justice. Many theorists caution against establishing firm definitions of Restorative Justice or setting standards for its practice, for fear of closing off innovation or responsiveness to local needs (Zehr & Toews, 2004). Many practitioners have made attempts to narrow the definition to meet the needs of their capacity in the community, schools, or other entities.

The overarching philosophy of Restorative Justice Restorative justice acknowledges that when a person does harm, it affects the person(s) they hurt, the community and themselves (University of Michigan, 2015). Restorative Justice in higher education resembles the models used in other American school systems where the use of this philosophy is an alternative approach to punitive policies.

Restorative Justice is utilized in the criminal and juvenile justice systems as an alternative approach to seek healing and restore relationships to as whole as possible. Daly (2002) mentions the political battles, such as the reconstruction of post-apartheid South Africa (p.57), which is utilized by many researchers to define the true essence of the global effectiveness of Restorative Justice.

Braithwaite (2003) describes restorative justice as not simply a way of reforming the criminal justice system, it is a way of transforming the entire legal system, our family lives, our conduct in the workplace and our practices of politics. Its vision is of holistic change in the way we do justice in the world. Restorative Justice de-centers the focus of criminal justice from the offender breaking a law of the state to the harm caused to the victim and community (Olson & Dzur, 2003). Restorative Justice offers victims and their supporters an opportunity to talk directly with wrongdoers, which is reactive in the sense that this form of justice seeks to rectify a wrong that has already occurred whether the responses are formal or informal. Restorative Justice provides a range of opportunities for dialogue, negotiation, and problem solving, whenever possible, which can lead to a greater sense of community safety, social harmony, and peace for all involved (Umbreit et al, 2005).

Restorative Justice requires, at minimum, that we address victims' harms and needs, hold offenders accountable to put right those harms, and involve victims, offenders, and communities in the process (Zehr, 2002, p. 25). Restorative Justice (RJ) concepts and practices have been used to resolve conflict in indigenous cultures, including the Maori people of New Zealand, Native American tribes in the U.S., and the Mayan people of Guatemala, for thousands of years (Pranis, 2005). Daly & Immarigeon (1998, p. 4) stated that in the early to mid-1970s is when the first victim-offender reconciliation programs were set up in Canada and the Midwestern U.S., and when few criminologists or practitioners were aware of indigenous justice traditions, the term Restorative Justice did not exist.

While Restorative Justice has been explained as a reactive measure, an alternative approach to the punitive systems across the world, restorative practices emerged to provide balance and equality to all shareholders; victims, offenders, and others. The most important function of criminal justice is to express social disapproval (Zehr & Toews, 2004, p. 50). In order to fully express social disapproval, all parties must have the opportunity to participate. Programs and practices deemed restorative consisted of: Prisoner Rights & Alternatives to Prisons, Conflict Resolution, Victim-Resolution, Victim Offender Reconciliation Programs (VORPs), Victim-Offender Mediation (VOM), Victim, Advocacy Family Group Conferences (FGCs), Sentencing Circles, and other practices (Daly & Immarigeon, 1998, pp. 6-11).

The aforementioned programs and/or practices were implemented in the 1970s (Daly & Immarigeon, 1998). The objective(s) was to bring closure via a facilitated process that included the victims and offenders. Supporters of the victim and offender were included in the process as well in cases where these parties were deemed to be a vital part of this process. As time progressed, professionals were included as a community resource in order to provide the needed assistance to an issue that was uncovered in the facilitated meeting.

RESTORATIVE PRACTICES

According to Daly & Immarigeon (1998, p. 4) victim-offender mediation, family group conferences, sentencing circles, victim impact panels, and other processes that are now called restorative evolved from different groups of people (often unknown to each other), who were experimenting with alternative practices. To provide an understanding of how restorative practices emerged prior to being coined a term, the practices mentioned frame the foundation for Talking Circles, one of many restorative practices use in a LLC.

The International Institute for Restorative Practices (IIRP), the world's first graduate school wholly devoted to restorative practices, distinguishes between the terms restorative practices and Restorative Justice; viewing Restorative Justice as a subset of restorative practices.

Restorative practices are a social science that studies how to build social capital and achieve social discipline through participatory learning and decision-making (Watchel, 2013) while Basar & Akan (2013) explain Restorative Justice as a positive discipline approach towards the search for sustainability in resolving conflicts which further support the claim of differentiating proactive and reactive measures.

Watchel (2013) provides a clear definition of Restorative Justice and practices:

Restorative justice is reactive, consisting of formal or informal responses to crime and other wrongdoing after it occurs. The IIRP's definition of restorative practices also includes the use of informal and formal processes that precede wrongdoing, those that proactively build relationships and a sense of community to prevent conflict and wrongdoing. Where social capital—a network of relationships—is already well established, it is easier to respond effectively to wrongdoing and restore social order—as well as to create a healthy and positive organizational environment.

Because this is an ever-changing global society, structure within education is imperative in terms of how services are delivered to the student. Educational and community leaders actively participate to connect academics and student development outside the classroom. According to the American Council on Education (1937), the development of students as whole persons interacting in social situations is the central concern of student personnel work and of other agencies of education.

The use of values, principles, and practices that Restorative Justice is built on forms the discussion and lessons surrounding the application of realistic situations. Therefore, students have the opportunity to apply philosophy to practice in all areas of their lives preparing them ample opportunities to integrate Restorative Justices' values, principles, and practices via assignments. Armour (2013) provides the space to learn how Restorative Justice relates to the students' chosen profession (even at an early age). A sense of moral agency resonates with each student participant. In this process of learning, students will change the frame of mind for their thought processes in order to transform and broaden their thinking. Admiration to reflective learning is noted in regards to a dominant pedagogy in professional development and adult education.

Karp (2013) notes that the Council for the Advancement of Standards in Higher Education argues that "Student Conduct Programs in higher education must enhance overall educational experiences by incorporating student learning and developmental outcomes in their mission." This applies to all levels of education in order to better prepare students transitioning into higher education. The literature on Restorative Justice and restorative practices are predominantly known within student conduct as a reactive measure while this research presents the paradigm shift to view restorative practices, in particular, Talking Circles as a proactive approach. The Student Discipline system of universities in many ways reflects the larger criminal justice system in the U.S. and is based on retributive justice (Darling, 2011, p. 3). Darling notes how higher education institutions have implemented Restorative Justice Principle and Practices in student conduct when a violation has occurred (pp. 6-8). Michigan State University employed restorative practices through a partnership between residence life and student life to help students and staff resolve conflict – to create a more holistic approach campus-wide (p. 8). At the same token, the University of Michigan created and distributed a 20-question survey tool where conference participants said the conference strengthened their sense of community (p.5). Although much emphasis has been placed on higher education, all levels of education can utilize restorative practices to provide the three concepts of The Balanced Approach. They are defined by the following: (1) accountability – creating an obligation for the offender to make amends; (2) building competencies – being more capable than when they entered as a rehabilitative goal; and (3) community safety – explicitly acknowledging and endorsing the responsibility to promote public safety and security.

We just covered quite a bit. Now, we will see how what we just covered affects our educational systems – the school-to-prison pipeline.

8

SCHOOL-TO-PRISON PIPELINE

Have you ever heard of the school-to-prison pipeline?
Please share your thoughts.

⊱⊰

**Without researching or using Google to find a response,
let's discuss.**

The pipeline is a connecting component between two
elements. In this case, the pipeline consists of the zero-
tolerance policies within the school system that tend to
remove a child from a structured environment and place
them into an unsupervised and sometimes unfortunate
situation. A child being ostracized or punished without
delving deeper into the who, what, when, why, and how's
does not provide equity or resolve. The second element is

the prison and/or juvenile [in] justice system that is "designed" to rehabilitate an individual after being accused of a crime, incarcerated, and sentenced to serve a questionable amount of time behind bars. To perpetuate the dynamics of the situation, incarceration could possibly extend to adulthood.

According to Owens (2017),

> *The School-to-Prison Pipeline is a social phenomenon where students become formally involved with the criminal justice system as a result of school policies that use law enforcement, rather than discipline, to address behavioral problems. A potentially important part of the School-to-Prison Pipeline is the use of sworn School Resource Officers (SROs), but there is little research on the causal effect of hiring these officers on school crime or arrests. Using credibly exogenous variation in the use of SROs generated by federal hiring grants specifically to place law enforcement in schools, I find evidence that law enforcement agencies learn about more crimes in schools upon receipt of a grant, and are more likely to make arrests for those crimes. This primarily affects children under the age of 15. However, I also find evidence that SROs increase school safety, and help law enforcement agencies*

make arrests for drug crimes occurring on and off school grounds.

I have questions I would like to pose at this time for open discussion:

1. Does either element provide restoration?

2. Are we seeking to punish in every situation?

3. Which crimes or harms do you consider punishable to the extent that incarceration is the only option?

4. Do you believe in diversion programs and/or the expungement process in order to remove the stigma associated with being deemed an ex-offender?

5. Have we become so numb to humanity that we place everyone in a one-size-fits all category?

9

A Punishment-to-Restoration Continuum

"Restorative discipline does not seek to deny consequences for misbehavior. Instead, it focuses on helping students understand the real harm done by their misbehavior, to take responsibility for the behavior, and to commit to positive change. We propose a continuum of discipline measures or choices in education, moving from punishment to consequences to solutions to restoration."

A Discipline Continuum

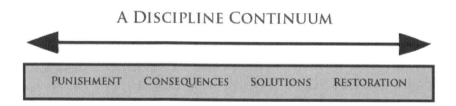

PUNISHMENT   CONSEQUENCES   SOLUTIONS   RESTORATION

Reference: Stutzman Amstutz, L. & Mullet, J.H. (2005) The Little Book Of Restorative Discipline for Schools: Teaching responsibility; creating caring climates. Good Books, Intercourse, PA.

10

Senate Bill 100 in the State of Illinois

August 24, 2015, Illinois Governor Rauner approved the Senate Bill 100 (SB 100) to curve the school conduct – school discipline measures taken which takes effect September 15, 2016. Many Illinois politicians are exhausted from the continuous misuse of discipline utilized in the current educational and societal circumstances. The influential political players have joined forces to ensure that schools place a prohibition on zero-tolerance policies. Due to political exhaustion, school administration must dissipate all other means of intervention before expelling students or suspending them for more than three days. School administration is tasked to make changes concerning: student discipline policies; parent-teacher advisory committee; and creation of memoranda of understanding with local law enforcement agencies that clearly define law enforcement role in schools. The educational context of the proverb, it takes a village to raise a child is more than a notion when involving all community shareholders.

This innovative opening to operative alternatives can be viewed as groundbreaking yet the philosophy of Restorative Justice (RJ) is a collaborative decision-making process that has been integrated as an alternative approach to historic means of justice systems globally for thousands of years (Walker, 2012). RJ has been used as an alternative measure to the ineffective zero-tolerance policy that plagues many of our children each school year. In the United States, the Truth and Reconciliation Commission of 1995 reflects the global effectiveness of RJ. The first victim-offender reconciliation programs surfaced in Canada and Midwestern U.S in the mid-1970s. Other program deemed restorative: Prisoner Rights & Alternative to Prisons, Conflict Resolution, Victim-Resolution, Victim Offender Reconciliation Programs, Victim-Offender Mediation, Victim Advocacy, Family Group Counseling, Sentencing Circles, and other practices.

From an educational perspective, RJ is similar to conflict
resolution. Conflict resolution is more ambitious as it tries
to affect the basic issues, the incompatibilities that direct
the conflicting parties (Wallensteen, 2015). RJ seeks to
resolve the issue(s) at hand to ensure that particular
incidents do not occur again while highlighting
accountability, (re)building relationships, and providing a
safe community. All shareholders directly affected have a
voice to speak from a safe place through a facilitated
process. Restorative Justice involves the utilization of
collaborative, community-based or community-oriented
techniques for responding to crimes and offenses (Karp,
2013) in this context, as an educational sanction to
violations of student code of conduct.

SENATE BILL 100 RECAP:

- Amends the school code; a prohibition on zero-
  tolerance policies

- Makes changes concerning:

- Student discipline policies

- Parent-teacher advisory committee

- Creation of memoranda of understanding with local law enforcement agencies that CLEARLY define law enforcement's role in schools

- Effective September 15, 2016

- Exhaust ALL other means of intervention before expelling students or suspending them for more than three days

- Restorative Justice (reactive) & Restorative Practices (proactive)

- Can eliminate the need for **some** zero tolerance policies

11

WHAT'S IN IT FOR SCHOOLS?

- Can decrease the need for suspensions

- Keeps students in school, students don't fall behind academically

- Builds a respectful school community

- Creates a caring community for students, teachers, and administrations

- Builds relationships between students and teachers

- Can be used for teaching appropriate behaviors

- Helps to develop competencies and skills

- Increases accountability of referred students

- Reduces recidivism

- Creates a healthy learning environment

Schools implementing restorative practices:

http://www.iirp.edu/pdf/IIRP-Improving-School-Climate-2009.pdf.

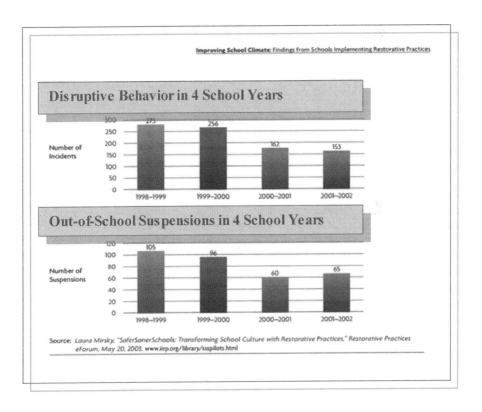

12

RESTORATIVE ENCOUNTER PRACTICES

This diagram describes RJ practices. Those within the large circle are encounter practices requiring specific training.

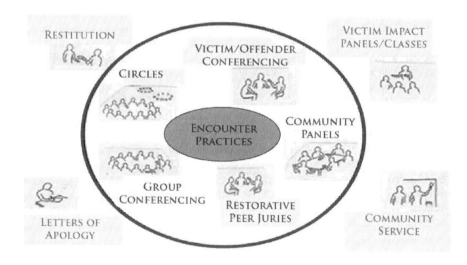

PRACTICES DEFINED:

- Victim/Offender Conferencing - Victim offender mediation is a process that provides interested victims an opportunity to meet their offender, in a safe and structured setting, and engage in a mediated discussion of the crime.

- Circles - Restorative Justice practices are used to address battles holistically and solve problems. Peace circles emphasize healing and learning through a collective group process, aiming to repair harm done with a standard of accountability.

- [Family] Group Conferencing - Family group conferencing involves the community of people most affected by the crime -- the victim and the offender; and the family, friends, and key supporters of both -- in deciding the resolution of a criminal incident.

- Restorative Peer Juries - Restorative Peer Juries are programs in which youth work together with youthful wrongdoers, victims and the community which is sometimes a school setting, to repair harm, build competencies and help to create safer schools and/or communities.

- Peer Mediation - Peer mediation constitutes an important part of conflict management strategies in schools. Many schools attempt to use peer intervention as a tool to teach positive conflict management. Peer mediation is one option that has shown to be successful at creating a feeling of peace and community in the schools it is utilized (Mason, 2014).

- Community Panels - A community restorative panel/board typically is composed of a small group of citizens, prepared for this function by intensive training, who conduct public, face-to-face meetings with offenders referred by police departments or courts to participate in the process.

13

CIRCLES

A Circle is a restorative practice that provides a safe, non-judgmental place to discuss issues of concern as a reactive approach and community building as a proactive approach.

CIRCLE STAGES:

- Getting acquainted
- Building relationships
- Addressing issue(s)
- Taking action

CIRCLE PROCESS:

- Seating arrangements – Circle format
- Opening ceremony – Create the respectful place of safety and to be mindful of the values
- Centerpiece – Central point placed on the floor in the center of the circle

- Values/guidelines – Speak without interruptions and commit to confidentiality
- Talking piece – Allows the speaker to speak without interruption; powerful equalizer (Pranis, 2005, p.8)
- Guiding questions – Goals of Talking Circle
- Closing ceremony – Application and awareness

TYPES OF CIRCLES:

- Support
- Talking
- Restorative Justice
- Sentencing
- Reentry
- School-based
- Domestic Violence
- Peacemaking
- Healing

CIRCLES HAVE THE OPPORTUNITY TO:

- Rehabilitate
- Understand interdependence
- Responsibility to one another

- Display how we all make immoral choices yet we are naturally good

CIRCLES INCLUDE:

- Meeting space – safe
- Talking Piece
- Keepers
- Ritual
- Consensus decision making

ABHOR THE SIN.

LOVE THE SINNER.

ৰ্কৰ্ক

"The Circle process allows participants to express their feelings freely, as long as they are respectful in how they do this. Yet, some adults are uncomfortable with students expressing feelings during a Circle. Sometimes they say, "I am not a social worker: or "I don't want to do any touchy-feely things; I teach."

Reference: Riestenberg, N. (2012). Circle in the Square: Building community and repairing harm in school. Living Justice Press, St. Paul, Minnesota.

14

Sample: Organizational Pilot Program (Schools)

Letter to Administration

The purpose of this program implementation is to spark conversation with the **administrator's name** led by **your name** with the intent to administer questionnaires to assess the current climate **provide further details** _____ .

The questionnaires will assist in identifying the need to implement Restorative Justice and Practices within **name of organization**, who is willing to participate in RJ training, and allow community members and other shareholders to be involved in the training process as well. The training for other shareholders was an added bonus for the RJ Program due to children needing balance between school, neighborhood/community, and home life. Allowing other shareholders to be trained in the restorative process enhances the effectiveness RJ has in the organization to reduce disciplinary infractions and increase attendance.

This program will build sustainability in the **name of organization, etc**. Once approved, the implementation of the RJ program, a tentative date will be scheduled for a time suitable for all shareholders to launch the pilot program. A formal letter was drafted from **your name** explaining the need for a pilot program that will flourish in to a sustainable mission along with statistical information from a valid source.

The letter submitted to **administrator's name** was followed with a letter to the shareholders that included consent forms and questionnaires. To answer any questions and/or concerns, please send emails to **your email address**.

Signature line, credentials, and contact information

Parent/Guardian Support Letter

I, **name and credentials,** who has a passion to **purpose**. There is a dire need to resolve student conflicts without removing a child from the school environment. Your involvement is one of the key components in supporting these efforts to resolve conflicts in an appropriate manner. A conflict between students affects other students not directly involved, the teacher, the school environment, parents/guardians, and the community for which the school is located. In essence, everyone is affected in some way.

The staff of **name of organization** provides an exceptional education to our children despite the conflicts that arise more frequently than usual. With the growing number of social media based conflicts (cyber bullying) and other methods of electronic based communication, the task to continue providing a quality education is becoming more stressful and difficult. It is not fair for our teachers to take a surmountable amount of time of each class to handle conflicts or disciplinary infractions. A prevention and intervention tool should be implemented to decrease disciplinary infractions, increase attendance, and build meaningful relationships amongst the students, parents/guardians, and staff of **name of organization**.

Restorative Justice (RJ) is a process of repairing harm that has been done. RJ emphasizes restoring a sense of well-being not only to those who were harmed, but to the individual who committed the harm and the surrounding community members. RJ in the schools gives way for the person harmed, the person who caused harm, and others indirectly involved an opportunity to resolve the issue(s) at hand without removing a student from the school environment. Note: All infractions do not prevent a child from being removed from the school environment (i.e. in-school/out-of-school suspension, expulsion).

Parental/Guardian support is needed in order for a Restorative Justice Incentive Program to be implemented; having a great impact in decreasing disciplinary infractions, increasing attendance, and building meaningful relationships as stated above. Once staff and nominated students are selected to complete Restorative Justice Facilitation Training, it is essential for our **name of organization** parents to be trained as well to offer a balance between the school and home environment. There is a questionnaire attached to this letter to gain an understanding of your knowledge on Restorative Justice and your availability for training.

Thank you for your time.

Signature line, credentials, and contact information

CONSENT FORM

Restorative Justice Pilot Program

I, _____ give **your name** permission to facilitate a pilot program in implementing Restorative Justice Practices at **name of organization** in an effort to decrease the suspension rate and increase productivity in the areas of: attendance, overall test scores, staff/student relationships, and strengthen the morale of the school environment.

The information collected during this pilot program will remain confidential and stored on school grounds in a secured location. If parents/guardians and/or staff would like to contact **your name and email address** at your convenience. All cases will be handled during school hours under the supervision of qualified staff. The pilot program conducted will follow all guidelines of **name of organization**.

_____   _____

Student Signature   Date

_____   _____

Parent/Guardian Signature   Date

_____   _____

RJ Coordinator Signature   Date

Restorative Justice Questionnaire (Staff)

1. Define Restorative Justice.

   _____

   _____

   _____

   _____

   _____

2. Is Restorative Justice needed in **name of organization**? _____

2A) If yes, why is Restorative Justice needed?

   _____

   _____

   _____

   _____

   _____

Would you be interested in Restorative Justice Training?
_____ Y _____ N

QUESTIONS	ONE	TWO	THREE OR MORE
How many students are reprimanded in your class?			
How many students are suspended?			
How much course work is covered?			
Once a student returns from suspension, how many assignments are incomplete or missing?			

RESTORATIVE JUSTICE QUESTIONNAIRE (PARENT/GUARDIAN)

1. Define Restorative Justice.

   _____

   _____

   _____

   _____

   _____

2. Is Restorative Justice needed in **name of organization**? _____

2A) If yes, why is Restorative Justice needed?

   _____

   _____

   _____

   _____

   _____

3. Would you be interested in Restorative Justice training opportunities for parents and/or guardians? Please check yes or no. _____ Y _____ N
   (if yes, answer question 5)

Please list dates and times of availability for training:

Sunday   From _____ am/pm to _____ am/pm

Monday   From _____ am/pm to _____ am/pm

Tuesday   From _____ am/pm to _____ am/pm

Wednesday   From _____ am/pm to _____ am/pm

Thursday   From _____ am/pm to _____ am/pm

Friday   From _____ am/pm to _____ am/pm

Saturday   From _____ am/pm to _____ am/pm

RESTORATIVE JUSTICE PILOT PROGRAM REFERRAL FORM

Student Name _____

ID # _____

Date of Birth _____

Age _____

Date of Incident _____

Date of Referral _____

Students Grade Point Average (GPA) _____

Referring Individual & Title

_____

Parties Involved

_____

_____

_____

Summary of Incident

_____

_____

_____

_____

_____

Student Signature   Date

_____   _____

RJ Coordinator Signature   Date

_____   _____

Administrator Signature   Date

_____   _____

Administrative Use Only

Of Absences in Current School Year_____

Of Visits to School Social Worker in Current School Year ____

15

PEER MEDIATION

STEPS IN PEER MEDIATION

1. Preamble: facilitator introduction of peer mediators, purpose, agenda, ground rules, and confidentiality (Peer Mediator #1)

2. Participants' stories: discussion of facts and discussion of impact on each other (Peer Mediator #2)

To the first youth:

- What happened? What were you thinking at that time?

- How have you been affected?

- How did you feel about this incident when it first happened? How do you feel about it now?

- Who do you think has been affected by what happened? In what way?

- What has been the hardest thing for you?

To the second youth:

- What happened? What were you thinking at that time?

- How have you been affected?

- How did you feel about this incident when it first happened? How do you feel about it now?

- Who do you think has been affected by what happened? In what way?

- What has been the hardest thing for you?

To the parents or supporters present:

- Tell us about how you first heard of this incident.

- What did you think at the time?

- What have you thought about it since?

- Whom do you think has been affected? In what way?

3. Repairing the harm: discussion and consensus
   agreement (Peer Mediator #1)

To the first youth:

- What do you need to make things right?

To the second youth:

- What do you need to make things right?

To the first and second youth:

- How can we make sure this does not happen again?

To the parents and supporters present:

- What do you think needs to be done to make things right?

- What needs to be done to make sure this does not happen again?

For peer mediators to consider:

- What do you think about these recommendations?

- Do they:

  - Hold the youth accountable for the harm that may have been caused?

  - Help the youth to make appropriate amends for what they did?

  - Assist them in building skills and competencies so that they do not repeat their behavior?

4. Closing and follow-up information (Peer Mediator #2)

- Summarize what was written on the agreement sheet.

- Ask each person present if they can agree to this contract?

- Have each person present sign the agreement sheet.

State that you would like to thank all for their contributions in dealing with this difficult matter. Acknowledgement is to be addressed for the way all shareholders worked through the issues. Explain that you look forward to seeing the report from the case manager/social worker that reflects completion of the agreement.

16

THE BALANCED APPROACH

- **Accountability** – understanding the extent of the harm caused. When you feel a part of the community, you are less likely to cause harm in that community.

- **Building Competencies** – skills to resolve issues for good instead of evil.

- **Community Safety** – competency development and accountability will assist in providing safety. Key word: community

17

THE SOCIAL DISCIPLINE WINDOW

HIGH ↑	

control (limit-setting, discipline)

TO punitive *authoritarian*	**WITH** restorative *authoritative*
NOT neglectful *irresponsible*	**FOR** permissive *paternalistic*

LOW — **support** (encouragement, nurture) → HIGH

This restorative approach confronts and disapproves of wrongdoing, while supporting and valuing the essential worth of the wrongdoer.

(Restorative Justice in Everyday Life: Beyond the Formal Ritual by Ted Watchel)

18

OLD AND NEW PARADIGM

Current (Traditional) Justice	Restorative Justice
Crime violates the state and it laws	Crime violates people and relationships
Justice focuses on establishing guilt	Crime violates people and relationships
Focus on past behavior – Did he or she do it?	Focus on the present and future
Accountability = Punishment	Accountability: understanding impact, repairing harm
One social injury replaced by another	Focus on repair of social injury
Community sidelined, represented by state	Community facilitates restorative process
Winner/loser conflict between adversaries	Encourage dialogue, mutual agreement
State action directed at offender – victim ignored	Victim, community, and offender all have direct roles
Rules and intent outweigh outcomes	Offender is responsible for behavior and repairs harm
Stigma of crime non-removable	Debt to victim and community
No opportunities for remorse or amends	Stigma of crime removable
	Possibilities for amends and expressions of remorse

19

RESTORATIVE QUESTIONS

1. What happened?
2. What was your part in what happened?
3. How did it happen?
4. What were you thinking at that time?
5. What have you thought since?
6. Who do you think was affected?
7. How were you affected?
8. How do you feel about what happened?
9. What was the harm caused?
10. Who do you think was harmed?
11. What needs to happen to make things as right as possible?
12. What do you need?
13. What do you think they need?
14. What are you willing to do to repair the harm that has been caused?
15. What needs to happen to solve this problem?
16. What is the right thing to do?

20

RESTORATIVE JUSTICE PREDICTIONS

- Restorative Justice practices improve community safety

- Restorative Justice practices encourage youth to be more empathetic

- Restorative Justice practices encourage youth to make amends for harmful, disrespectful, or law breaking behavior

- Restorative Justice practices reduce school problems

- Restorative Justice practices increase positive youth outcomes

- Restorative Justice practices increase victim satisfaction with the justice system/process

- Restorative Justice practices increase victim restitution

- Restorative Justice practices reduce disproportionate minority contact (with the juvenile justice system)

21

A Journey Not Shared is a Soul Not Healed
Dr. Shaniqua Jones

"In all social situations, our narratives are an essential aspect of living restoratively because, by telling our story, we not only develop deeper sense of self, but also expand and deepen our connectedness to each other."

(Zehr & Toews, 2004, p. 392)

෨෨

22

REFERENCES

American Council on Education. (1937). *The student personnel point of view*. Washington, DC: Author.

Armour, M. (2013). Real-World Assignments for Restorative Justice Education. Contemporary Justice Review, 16(1), 115-136. doi:10.1080/10282580.2013.769300

Basar, M., & Akan, D. (2013). Assessment of class teachers' dispute resolution applications in

conflict environments on the basis of restorative justice. International Journal of Academic

Research, 5(5), 26-30. doi:10.7813/2075-4124.2013/5-5/B.4

Braithwaite, J. (2004). Restorative Justice and De-professionalization. The Good Society, 13(1), 28-31.

Daly, K. (2002). Restorative Justice The Real Story. *Punishment & Society*, 4(1), 55-79.

Daly K. and R. Immarigeon (1998) "The Past, Present, and Future of Restorative Justice: Some Critical Reflections." The Contemporary Justice Review 1 (1): 21-45.
Hutchinson, M. S. (2000). Restorative Justice, Voluntary Action and Social Capital: A Perspective From Northern Ireland. In *The Fourth International Conference of The International Society for Third Sector Research.*

Darling, J. (2011). *Restorative Justice in Higher Education: A Compilation of Formats and Best Practices.* University of San Diego.

English Oxford Living Dictionaries. (2016). Retrieved from: https://en.oxforddictionaries.com/definition/respect

Illinois Balanced and Restorative Justice (2016). Home. Retrieved from: http://www.ibarji.org/default.asp

Karp, D. (2013). The Little Book of Restorative Justice for Colleges and Universities. Intercourse, PA: Good Books.

Mason, W. (2014). Peer mediation as a form of conflict resolution (Doctoral dissertation, EASTERN OREGON UNIVERSITY).

Merriam-Webster. (2016). Retrieved
from https://www.merriam-webster.com/dictionary/values

Owens, E. G. (2017). Testing the School-to-Prison
Pipeline. Journal of Policy Analysis and Management,
36(1), 11-37

Pranis, K. (2005) Circle Processes. Intercourse, PA: Good
Books.

Riestenberg, N. (2012). Circle in the Square: Building
community and repairing harm in school. Living Justice
Press, St. Paul, Minnesota.

Stutzman Amstutz, L. & Mullet, J.H. (2005) The Little
Book Of Restorative Discipline for Schools: Teaching
responsibility; creating caring climates. Good Books,
Intercourse, PA.

Truth and Reconciliation Commission. (2003). Promotion
of National Unity and Reconciliation Act 34 of 1995.
Retrieved
from http://www.justice.gov.za/legislation/acts/1995-
034.pdf

Umbreit, M.S., Vos, B., Coates, R.B., & Lightfoot, E.
(2005). Restorative Justice in the Twenty-First Century: A

Social Movement Full of Opportunities and Pitfalls, 89, 251.

University of Michigan (2016). Retrieved from: https://oscr.umich.edu/article/restorative-justice-circles

Walker, L. (2012). Restorative justice today: Practical applications. Sage.

Wallensteen, P. (2015). Understanding conflict resolution. Sage.

Watchel, Ted. (2013) Defining Restorative. Creative Commons AttributionShareAlike 3.0.

Zehr, H., & Toews, B. (2004). *Critical Issues in Restorative Justice*. Monsey, NY: Criminal Justice Press.

Zehr, H. (2002). *The Little Book of Restorative Justice*. Intercourse, PA: Good Books.

23

<u>Notes</u>

_____

_____

_____

_____

_____

_____

_____

_____

NOTES

_____

_____

_____

_____

_____

_____

_____

_____

_____

_____

_____

_____

_____

Notes

_____

_____

_____

_____

_____

_____

_____

_____

_____

_____

NOTES

_____

_____

_____

_____

_____

_____

_____

_____

_____

_____

_____

Notes

NOTES

NOTES

NOTES

_____

_____

_____

_____

_____

_____

_____

_____

_____

_____